KING
OF THE
RING

Benny "The Jet"

KING OF THE RING

How To Use Your Gym Equipment and Other Tricks Of The Trade

By Benny "The Jet" Urquidez

Pro-Action Publishing

A Division of Pro-Action Sports, Inc.

P.O. Box 26657, Los Angeles, CA 90026

A NOTICE OF CAUTION AND DISCLAIMER

Neither the author nor the publisher assumes any responsibility for the use or misuse of information contained in this book. The illustrations and text in this book are for entertainment purposes only. Any injury or injuries which may result from such acts are solely the responsibility of the reader.

In the event the reader practices any of the training techniques in this book, he does so at his own risk. These karate techniques should be studied and practiced only under the guidance of a qualified instructor. A minor should not practice any of the training techniques in this book unless he has parental approval and is under the guidance of a qualified instructor.

Before beginning any type of physical exercise, including anything demonstrated in this book, the reader should be examined by his physician and given a clean bill of health.

Other fine titles from PRO-ACTION Publishing
GRAPPLING MASTER Combat for Street Defense and Competition by Gene LeBell
KARATE DYNAMICS – The Ukidokan System by Benny "The Jet" Urquidez
THE ORIGINAL MARTIAL ARTS ENCYCLOPEDIA: Tradition - History – Pioneers by John Corcoran and Emil Farkas

Editor: STUART SOBEL
Art Director: DANILO J. SILVERIO
Cover Photo and inside photo techniques: JAIMEE ITAGAKI
Make-up for cover photo : SARA URQUIDEZ
Assisting Benny Urquidez is MICHAEL MORTEO

Other books by Benny Urquidez:
Training and Fighting Skills (Unique Publications)
Karate Dynamics: The Ukidokan System (Pro-Action Publishing)

Printed in the United States of America
ISBN No: 0-9615126-4-4
Library of Congress Catalog Card Number: 94-069739

Dedication

To the three women in my life. My wife Sara who is my friend, my lover and my partner. My daughter Monique whom I feel very blessed to have. To the memory of my Mother, who will always be my hero.

Notice: In order to understand the terms **Chess Player** and **Checker Player** as well as to get the maximum benefit from KING OF THE RING it is necessary for you to read the Introduction. Thank you! *The Editor*

Table of Contents

OLYMPIC AUDITORIUM
UNITED STATES CONTACT KARATE
Championships

URQUIDEZ-HANSON PRESENTS

FULL CONTACT KARATE

Benny's first playbill cover circa 1975. "From the time I could remember, whenever there was something that had to be done and there was only enough money in the family for one of us to do it, everyone would put their money in a hat to fund that person. That person was generally me. I was usually the one to fight". See Introduction. This show was the precursor to the organizing of the World Karate Association (WKA), a major sanctioning body begun by Arnold Urquidez and Howard Hanson.

Foreword

f I were a singer, and Luciano Pavarotti approached me to give a helpful tip, you'd better believe I'd play attention. And when I'm out on the golf course, where I really need help, and a Hall-of-Famer like Jack Nicklaus offered to show me, I'd hang on his every word.

Each field, all professions and every walk of life has its Pavarottis and Nicklauses. Greatness comes to but a precious, select few. A blessing to an individual, touched by the hand of God.

That blessing touched Benny Urquidez, and as such he has become the foremost competitor, authority, spokesman, teacher and guru in the arena of full-contact competition and hand-to-hand combat. *'Cara a cara y mano a mano'*, nobody does it better than Benny "The Jet". Nobody knows it better than Benny "The Jet". Nobody teaches it better than Benny "The Jet".

Of my 20 years in professional boxing, I've traveled the world watching men and women match will and skill. The first 13 years I did so as a writer and sportscaster. Since 1988 I've done so as a commissioner. I've seen wrestling in Mexico, Muay Thai in Bangkok, kick-boxing in Seoul and boxing at home in the United States and virtually everywhere else in the world. Despite my global tours and tens-of-thousands of full-contact contests viewed, I have still not come across that one book which encompasses the entire scope of what it means to be a full contact competitor. Of what it takes to be a full contact competitor. Of how to train and prepare mentally, physically and spiritually as a full contact competitor - until now. Until Benny "The Jet": *KING OF THE RING: How To Use Your Gym Equipment and Other Tricks of The Trade.*

Like "The Jet" himself, this book is in a class by itself. Because of his incredible knowledge and expertise in every facet of the Martial Arts. Benny is able to walk us through the book as if he is standing by our side, gently, patiently and professionally explaining every detail with his soft, almost hypnotic voice.

During my two decades in boxing, I have never had as many aspects of full contact competition explained as clearly and as thoroughly as Benny explains in this book. Had it been around when I was boxing, well who knows. However, it's here now and we can all thank him for taking the time to put his knowledge on paper.

Between covers, "the Jet" explains it all. This book is a veritable smorgasbord of fistic delights. It's kind of an "Everything You Always Wanted To Know About Full Contact Sports But Nobody Had Any Answers to Your Questions Until Now", type of book.

From something as seemingly "simple" as hitting the bag to the easy-looking and oh so important job of wrapping the hands. Benny "The Jet" guides us, like a private tutor, through every facet of the world of full contact competition.

How instructional is this book? I asked three young New York boxers to wrap their hands for me. None of the three came close to wrapping their mitts correctly. Then I showed them a tape of Benny "The Jet" teaching and explaining the proper way to wrap the hands, just the way he does in this book. The three young boxers again wrapped their hands. This time, each did it to perfection.

If it's headgear you're concerned with or sparring gloves which connect with that headgear, Benny Urquidez covers it thoroughly in this book. If you're wondering about the proper mouthpiece for you, or mouth guard (they're called gum shields in England), Benny covers them too. He delves into the purpose for each piece of work-out equipment along with the ring entrance, ring strategy as well as a testing methjod which he calls 'The Boxer's Walk' and so much more that you'll delight in its breadth and scope. Urquidez talks to both the recreational beginner right up to the serious professional.

We all have books which just sit on the shelf for years and years, taken out only to be dusted every time Halley's Comet appears. Benny "The Jet", *KING OF THE RING* will be that one book you will never have to dust.

I truly believe you've made a wise investment. Owning and using this book is like having Benny "The Jet" training you and worlking your corner. What a winning combination.

RANDY GORDON
Chairman, New York State Athletic Commission and
Boxing Analyst

INTRODUCTION

ighters come in many weights, styles, and abilities. However, when it comes to types of fighters, there are only two. I describe them as either a **Checker Player** or a **Chess Player**. A Checker Player will take a hit to give a hit. He will even take three and four hits to get one in. This type is also known as a brawler. He generally enters the sport with a lot of anger and bitterness for the way he may have been treated in his life. He is looking for a release. He is so focused that even if he gets a brutal beating it will not deter him. This is the Mike Tyson/Dennis Alexio style of fighter.

The Checker Player can become very good as well as very dangerous, but it is debatable whether he will last. Those hits, even though they may be "ignored" still take their toll. Sometimes a Checker Player will make it to the pros without sustaining major damage, and sometimes a promising career will be cut short because of taking too many hits. This type of fighter never really becomes "the people's choice". They are too angry to develop a public persona that would lend itself into a commercial public recognition and product endorsement.

As the Checker Player progresses he can get cocky. If he is smart he can turn that cockiness into a gain by developing a winning personality if he realizes that he doesn't have to take the punishment. He can also continue to be the brawler and do such damage to himself that he can no longer continue. The exception is the physical fighter who is smart. He changes from a Checker Player to a Chess Player, a thinker, a showman.

The Chess Player is a strategist in the science of the sport. He would rather give a four-five-six and not have to take a hit. He will use technique, combination and blocking principles in order to throw leather and hit the target. He enters the ring more for the curiosity, to see if he can really match tangible wits with his opponent. This is the Peter "Sugarfoot" Cunningham/Sugar Ray Leonard style of fighter. This is the type of fighter that builds a sport.

The most obvious type of likeable personality in boxing is George Foreman or in kick-boxing it is Bill "Superfoot" Wallace and Don "The Dragon" Wilson. Everyone likes them. You see, boxing and kick-boxing is like every other sport and that is it's all show business. The Olympics is show business, baseball is show business and Broadway is show business. Whenever you need an audience to complete the cycle, it's show business. The crowd has to like you or hate you for you to keep them coming back for more.

The Chess Player begins his career out of curiosity and enters the ring as a panic survivor. He is very quick. He wants to last and because of this survival instinct, he will show combinations and rapid movement that translates into a showman.

You might wonder what happens when a brawler, a Checker Player, and a Chess Player steps into the ring. A classic example was the Sugar Ray Leonard/Roberto Duran bout. The infamous "no mas" event. Leonard frustrated the worthy Duran to such an extent that Duran just threw up his hands in disgust and walked out of the ring during an early round. The mental always has the advantage over the physical.

The one equalizing element that both types of fighters share when they enter the ring is fear. You won't find many that will admit to it, but take it from me this is fact.

There are some that fear being hurt or embarrassed. There are some that fear that they won't live up to their fans, friends and family expectation. Before I realized this I had to do a lot of soul searching on the subject. I felt that since I didn't fear man, what kind of fear did I have? I couldn't figure it out. I only knew it was so.

From the time I could remember, whenever there was something that had to be done and there was only enough money in the family for one of us to do it, everyone would put their money in a hat to fund that person. That person was generally me. I was usually the one to fight and the family's money would be riding on it. This went way back to my point fighting days. My fear was letting them down. Later my fear was in disappointing my family, friends and fans in not putting on a good show. I never wanted that to happen.

The ring, in all instances, can translate into real life. Everything that happens within the four wall of the ropes is for real. There is no escape. It is the true test. You either stand or fall on your own ability. There is also the fear of the unknown. Not knowing how you will do in combat. The way you present yourself is the way you are treated by your opponent, just as in life. You are praised for your ability and shunned for a lack of courage. Character and integrity, desire, self esteem and future goals are all wrapped up in your performance, but not necessarily in the outcome of the bout. And the only "easy" exit a fighter can take is to lay down and be counted out. The same as it is in life.

To me, the ring is my home. If you are invited over to someones home you are always on your best behavior. You ask permission to get a drink of water, to use the bathroom, or to use the phone. That is proper and acceptable. However in my own home I can put my feet up on the furniture and that is proper too, because it is my home.

You might notice that when I get into the ring I'm very relaxed. I greet my opponent with a little smile. My perception is that I am welcoming him into my home. He is my guest whether I am in his country or he is in mine. I always try to be the perfect host. I don't have to give a stone face or a glare. A relaxed, calm presence and a little smile can be more disarming than any mugging you might do for your opponent or to the camera.

Someone who isn't wasting his energy in kicking up dust as a bull does before he charges will appear to be in perfect control and his least concern is his opponent. Can you imagine what an opponent feels when he comes in contact with such serene confidence. I can see subtle as well as obvious changes in his demeanor.

We've been talking about the competitor as more or less the other person. Let's personalize this and talk specifically about you. What I am about to do is to take you into your workshop, perhaps for the first time. I'm not talking about the gym, that is the physical part of your training. That's is a given. You have to train for the physical side of the sport. I won't get any resistance with that. The other is more personal for both me and for you.

You see, we all play mind games to psych us up for the task ahead. There are mind games to try and fool ourselves into believing that we are the best when we honestly know that we are not. Then there is the other type of mind game. That is the game of projection played with an honest deck.

I'll let you inside my workshop and show you around. The workshop is the mind. Inside my workshop I close the door. It is sealed against any negative thoughts. No self-doubt nor concern can enter. It is filled with strong talent and beautiful gifts.

On one wall of my workshop I see a movie screen. I am the writer-star-director of my own film. I can see myself performing whatever I have to do in a hero-like quality that surpasses anything that has ever been on film. It is my decision on what goes on the screen. On another wall I have all of my tools, everything for the workout. There is nothing lacking. I use each tool for its designed purpose at the maximum it can be used. I do not hold back. On another wall is wardrobe. It is the persona of my choosing and I dress the part. On the fourth and final wall is the door to the outside world. I can tip-toe out the door and see if the coast is clear before I exit my work shop. Or I can go out of the door as a gladiator with my hand on my sword ready to be drawn. It is my choosing. It is the way people perceive you when you enter a room or enter the ring. It take five seconds to form a first impression and five years to reverse it. So you might as well do it correctly the first time.

Think about your reasons for wanting to step into the ring. It will help your confidence and make your purpose clear. You see there are a lot easier ways of getting fame and making money. A person can record a song in their garage one week and the next week it can be a number one hit. An "actor" with no experience can make a movie and end up winning the Academy Award for Best Actor. It is luck and timing.

In the fight game this can never happen. It cannot be a fluke. There are too many tests and contenders along the way for someone to be crowned World Champion not to have the actual talent. It is the truest form in displaying talent that you will ever find. There is no teammate to rely on. It is you against someone equally matched. You are really the modern day gladiator.

Don't be discouraged if you don't get this method down right away. I've had seasoned pros have a problem at first. It's only because what I am teaching you is a new way of approaching your work-out.

If you catch yourself thinking negative thoughts, stop it immediately. You can be your own worst enemy. However you approach your training, whether it be with frustration, awkwardness or fear, it's okay. Just don't put yourself down for it. You have to allow yourself the luxury to make mistakes if you want to become great. You can learn from them.

The secret is to relax and have fun with it. Your body will figure it out. Your body will find it's own rhythm and timing. Your body will become stronger and adjust to the stepped-up pace. You just have to give yourself permission to enjoy it. Because when you enjoy something you become very interested. You become more aware of what you are doing and less focused on what you are feeling.

Fighters have various reasons for wanting to jump into the ring. Whatever your reason it should be a passionate reason because the sport is too hard to do on a whim. Some people want the fame and some want the money. Most want both and that's fine, but there should to be more to it.

Fame and money should not be your sole motivating factor. There has to be more. For me it is the excitement of the ring. It is the love of competition. It is the most revealing form of hard earned talent and raw courage that you can ever find. There is no one to back you up. It can be a revealing look at yourself.

Now, what does all of this have to do with training with your gym equipment. Everything and more. You see, whether you play this as a game of physical checkers or physical chess, the equipment is all used in the same manner.

What I'm showing you is a circuit. It is to instruct you on how to use every bag at your disposal, and to encourage you to use them in the order presented in King Of The Ring.

Notice that we begin with sparring in the ring. In this case we are showing ring strategy. You want to get your sparring over with first because you are your sharpest and freshest at this point. Then you go from your lighter equipment to your progressively heavier equipment for your workout.

Toward the end of your training session you will note that I go back to the lighter piece of equipment, the speed bag. The reason for this is after your workout your arms are very tired. You cannot work the speed bag unless you keep your hands up. Most fighters have a tendency to drop their hands (their defense) when their arms get tired. Along with all of the other benefits to this exercise it will train you to keep your hands up when you are tired. I truly believe that the way you train is the way you react. In the ring you don't have time to think, only react.

The last of the workout in this session is the jump rope. This is a cool down for your muscles all the while it keeps your heart rate up.

The use of the equipment is the routine. By studying this method you will get the maximum benefit from each workout session.

Most of the bags that you see in my workout I've designed. You won't find them in too many gyms, yet. However, whatever type of bag you might have you can create the same kind of workout benefit.

The Upper-Cut Bag; the Banana Bag with the donut ring or Saturn ring; the Power Shield; the Body Bag; just to name a few, I've created for myself and my students. But don't let the lack of a specific bag stop you from your workout.

Most gyms will usually just have an 80 pound-four foot bag. You can use all of the techniques that you learn here on that one bag depending upon the impact that you use.

A stinging or slapping impact occurs when a technique is snapped or controlled. You experience this type of impact in traditional karate tournaments where a move is pulled short of maximum effect.

The other types of impact that you will experience in the ring are a shattering impact and a breaking impact. A shattering impact shocks the body, but it doesn't move the body from its planted position. The technique is snapped similar to the way a stinging impact is snapped. A breaking impact utilizes a follow-through technique. That kind of impact will move the body either backward or to the side, depending on what you want to accomplish. You might, for example, deliver a combination of a shattering impact and a breaking impact. One is to shock your opponent's body without moving him and the other is to finish him off with a breaking impact.

In King Of The Ring I will tell you the type of impact to use with each piece of equipment. If you have to improvise then use the same impact that is described for whatever bag you have to use.

Training is not meant to be entertaining, but it can be fun if you approach it with the proper attitude. Train to exceed your potential. Don't short change yourself with your workout. You will know if you have instantly when you step into the ring for real and look over at your opponent. Make each training session meaningful. Learn something new each time and realize your growth.

Don't do these workouts in a vacuum. Really think about what you are doing and how each piece of equipment complements the other. Understand the purpose of each piece of equipment and approach it in that spirit.

A beginner will generally take two hours to run through this session. The better you get the faster the workout. A pro will take an hour. The reason for this is that even though the pro will be doing longer times on each piece of equipment, he will go from equipment to equipment without having to wait for recovery time. The new fighter and the amateur will not be able to keep up the same pace because recovery time is longer. Once you get use to it you will find your workout time getting shorter.

Whether you are a Checker Player or a Chess Player I salute you. You have my respect. As for me, I personally enjoy a game of physical chess. My toughest opponent was another chess player whom I knocked out in four rounds, but I still consider Kunimatsu Okao my finest opponent. I give him all the respect. He really put me on my game. To him and to all the opponents whom I've met in the ring, I want to sincerely thank you for a great time. I remember you all. You've helped me grow as a fighter and a person. I can never repay you for that great life experience.

I've officially retired from competition, but the ring is still my home. It is where my heart is, the place I feel the most comfortable. In 1993, at the age of 41, I hung up my gloves from competition. I wanted to retire the same way I always fought, with a furry and speed of a jet fighter. With an undefeated record (57-0 with 49 knock-outs) many friends and family told me not to do it. They didn't want to see my record blemished. I, on the other hand, didn't want to be a prisoner of my record. I wanted the opportunity to see if I still had what it took. To me I was very excited about jumping back into the ring for one last hurrah.

Since Japan had given me so much opportunity during my career, I wanted to return the favor and fight the best Japan had to offer. Yoshihisa Tagami, a twenty-five year old with a 22-0 record was to be the chosen guest in my home. He didn't disappoint me or the crowd. This colorful kick-boxer proved to be a worthy opponent. I was glad that I got the nod and bumped the record to 58-0, but that was only the icing on the cake as far as I was concerned.

The joy for me was just getting back into the ring again and mixing it up with someone that wanted so badly to take the title from me and bring it back to Japan from where I originally took it. You see, being the first American to win a kick-boxing title in Japan against their top, and up until that time, undefeated champion I feel demands a responsibility in offering someone from that country a chance to win it back for the last time.

In conclusion, I have worlds of experience and much advise that you will see in this book, King of the Ring. However, as far as the type of competitor I would recommend for any young up and coming fighter, be a Chess Player, you'll always be glad you did. Check mate!

BENNY 'THE JET' URQUIDEZ

CHAPTER ONE

Entering The Ring

Through The Ropes

There are three different ways of entering the ring. The most preferred entrance is through the ropes. This is the serious fighter. He can be both the Chess and the Checker Player (refer to Introduction for an explanation). All of the greats, the champions go through the ropes. They are very determined.

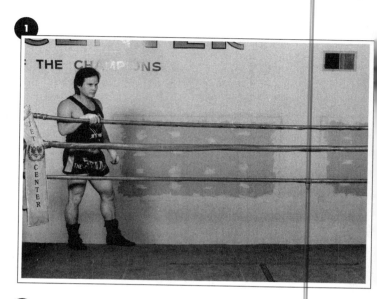

Over The Ropes

Same champion, same kind of fighter, however they hide their fear. They tell the audience that they will give a show. They do it as a cover-up. They have fear, but they cover it with a bravado.

Under The Ropes

The Checker Player wants to do something different with a cockiness, showing the unexpected. The Chess Player reassures the audience that he's different.

The Checker Player always thinks on the spot. The Chess Player will practice his entrance so that he is smooth. It projects an assured entrance and a confident image. A Checker Player doesn't do his homework other than train. A Chess Player considers every detail important. He plans his entrance to what he will wear. The image is as important to him as the competition. The one characteristic all fighters share is that they never take their eyes off their opponent.

2

4

The Referee's Instructions

The psyching out of your opponent begins with entering the ring and continues with the referee's instruction. This is how you can tell what your opponent is feeling, whether he realizes it or not. The opponent will do one of three things.

He will look at you regardless if the ref is talking to him and will give you the hard stare. He is trying to psych you into believing he's out for the kill. Inexperienced fighters can melt with this kind of passive-aggressive behavior.

He'll look at the referee and not at you regardless whether the ref is looking at you or him. He doesn't want to look at you. He doesn't have much confidence in himself.

He'll look at the ground whether the ref is look at you or him. He has no confidence at all and is showing his fear.

Tap Gloves. Some fighters like to do a hard up and down, or a hard push. I do a light tap without revealing anything. Sometime I'll sneak a little thumb jab into my opponent's solar plexus as he is walking away. I'll give him a little wink and a smile and wish him luck. A light tap on the solar plexus, especially unexpected can take the wind out of the most confident warrior. And with a smile and a wink it won't upset the referee.

A lesson to be learned is that a person is never safe, even when he is being given referee's instructions. You can study your opponent and take the heart out of him before you hear the first round bell sound.

My method is to not give any hard stare and not to give a neutral stare. My intent is to give a picture of complete comfort, relaxation and excitement. I look upon the ring as my home and I am inviting the opponent into my home.

You see, when someone is invited into your home, you have the advantage. They are on their best behavior. They ask permission to remove their coat, to have a drink of water and to use the bathroom. On the other hand, I don't have to ask their permission for anything. I am really at home. I can put my feet on the furniture and not be rude or offensive because it is my home.

My mind-set is that this ring is my home. I am comfortable and relaxed and I'm looking forward to the competition. In my home I am always the perfect host.

CHAPTER TWO

Testing The Ring With The Boxer's Walk

A few hours before a show, after the ring has been put up and forgotten, I like to get a chance to spend a few minutes inside. I like to test it. To see where the strengths and weaknesses lie-in-wait of this newly erected square jungle. I go through a series of testing patterns which I call The Boxers Walk.

The Boxer's Skip

Feet together - right leg - feet together - left leg - feet together - right leg, all done with rhythm and a little bounce as if your skipping rope. What you're doing here is determining whether there are any soft spots on the floor. Where there are you want to stay away from that area.

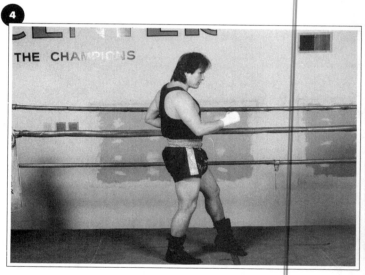

Moving Side To Side

See if there are any gaps in the canvas. If the seams are overlapped or seamless. You don't want to trip over a seam. You do this by using a shuffle, sliding your shoes over the mat. Sometimes you can't see a seam on top of the mat, but you feel one underneath. You'll feel a bulge. You don't want to trip over a seam, so you can detect these land minds by performing this shuffle.

Half Moons

This gives you an indication of the texture of the canvass by pivoting. You can find out if it's sticky or slippery so you don't twist an ankle when you turn. Sometime the advertising logo that is silk-screened in the center of the ring can get slippery.

Being the main event I always fight last. I know the floor will usually be wet in the two corners. With all of the fights that come before mine I have to be aware that the floor is going to be very dirty. Your trainer should look out for this and point out any trash that may have been thrown into the ring and wasn't picked up by the referee or if any water hadn't been wiped up from a previous bout.

Testing The Ropes

You go against the ropes to test if they're tight or loose. You want a little give to it, but not too much or you could go over the top. Also, don't always assume that there is rope underneath the wrapping. I fought more than once where there was dock cable that was used. You have to know these things so you can protect yourself from surprises.

Hitting The Corners

See if there are any buckles or bolts that happen to be protruding. You want to know which corners to stay away from.

With all of this testing it prepares you for the ring. You will know every squeak and soft spot when you get through. The primary reason for this is so you know where the hidden dangers of the ring are located so you can avoid them.

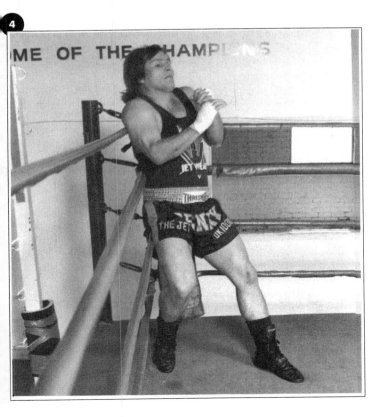

Secondarily, this will tell you where you want to place your opponent. If there is a soft spot in the ring, get him to that area. If you plan to put your opponent into the corner, and you have a choice as to which corner, why not put him into the one that is the least comfortable, which will also give him something else to worry about.

Once I get into the ring for fight night, I usually give one last test that is not obvious, just to see if anything has changed. Never assume anything!

Ring Position

Without a question the best place to be is the center of the ring. You've got room to move with no interference. The worst place to find yourself is in a corner. The ropes are the second worse place, but at least there is some give. If the ropes are too loose you can fall over the top. However, since you've already tested the ropes you know how much you can rely on them. If you are in your opponent's corner or in your own you will generally find a lot of water, so if you have your opponent in one of these corners you have to be aware that the floor may be slippery and not rely on the corner for leverage.

Run The Ring

When you run the ring you are using the ropes to your advantage. Grip the rope to change direction quickly. You can use it to shift in different directions and therefore confuse your opponent as to your position. The first series of photos are for practicing by yourself.

2

4

The second series of photos is for practicing with an opponent.

2

4

Bouncing Off The Ropes.

Bouncing off the ropes and learning how to pivot either left or right.

Getting Out of a Corner.

Getting out of a corner by weaving and then getting your opponent against the corner is the strategy. This is a defensive move. Your opponent shoots a right. You weave under his right arm pivoting on your left foot ending up behind him.

2

Keeping your opponent against the ropes.

He moves to the left. You step-drag to the left. He moves to the right and you step-drag to the right. This is known as cutting the corners.

2

4

CHAPTER THREE

The Focus Gloves

The purpose of the focus gloves are for eye-hand coordination. The gloves are moving targets. The trainer is making up the target areas spontaneously and the fighter reacts. There is no time to think, only to react.

The benefit of the focus gloves is that you can use various hand combinations in a moving position. It forces you to work on timing and target areas. It also makes you bob and weave. It improves body blocking and hitting what you see on target.

Hear it through commands. See it as a target. Feel it when you make contact. These are the hand combinations to perfect your techniques.

All training exercises should be by rounds numbers and minutes. Rounds are always based on three minutes rounds with a one minute rest period. Even though kick-boxing is a two minute round you should train for a three minute round.

For the focus gloves the new fighter and the amateur should do three rounds and the pros four to five rounds.

Jab-right cross-left hook

2

Left hook-right cross-left hook

2

Feint down-jab-over-hand right

Right cross-left hook-right cross

2

Right uppercut-left hook

Right cross-left hook to the body-left hook to the head-overhand right

Jab-drag step-right upper cut-overhand right

Feint down jab-overhand right

Bob right-right uppercut-over-hand right

Feint down-right cross to the body-right upper cut-over-hand right

Feint down-right  to the body-right upper cut

2

4

Bob left-left upper cut-right upper cut-spinning elbow

2

3

5

Spinning back fist

2

Left hook-right cross

Body block
right-left hook

2

Body block left-right cross

1

2

Parry front elbow-parry-back elbow

Parry-back elbow

Parry-spinning back fist

2

Parry-left hook

2

Parry-right cross

Parry-jab

1

Feint down-jab

2

Feint back-right cross

Opponent (trainer) shoots a right cross, you weave to your left. He shoots a left hook, your weave to your right

Bob left-left upper cut

2

Bob right-right uppercut

Bob right-overhand right

1

2

Bob left-left hook to the body

FOCUS GLOVES WITH A BODY PROTECTOR

With the Body Protector you can hit to the body with impact. The trainer is able to give more combinations to the kick-boxer by using knees, shins and feet.

Skip ball kick.

1

2

Skip ball kick-right cross to the body-left hook to the body.

Back knee to the body.

1

CHAPTER FOUR

The Power Shield

The Power Shield is designed for the kick-boxer in working target areas with a moving position. You develop moving combinations and impact. Power can be developed low and high without injury to your trainer or to yourself. This is used only for kicking, no punching. You can use it to maneuver the Power Shield to kick it, either to the left or the right.

Amateurs work for three rounds. Pros for four to five rounds.

Outside sweep, hitting the calf.

2

Inside sweep kicking the inside of the calf.

Power round house kick to the body-shuffle back-inside thigh kick.

2

Outside thigh kick-inside power round kick to the body.

2

4

Outside body kick-switch-inside body kick.

2

4

Cross rear heel kick.

Jump-spinning back kick.

Switch-spinning wheel kick

Switch-side kick.

2

Back-side kick.

2

Front-side kick.

1

2

Feint down-jump front round house kick.

Jump-round
house kick.

2

Feint down-front jump ball kick.

2

Jump ball kick.

1

Ball kick-switch-ball kick.

2

4

Switch axe kick.

2

4

Jump-side kick.

Jump-front spinning back kick.

2

4

Switch-spinning wheel kick.

2

4

Spinning wheel kick.

Jump-front side kick.

Spinning back kick.

Jump-side kick.

2

CHAPTER FIVE

Thai Pads

Originating in Thailand for the Muay Thai competitors, the pads have found their way throughout the world for any kick-boxer that fights international rules which allow leg kicks.

This piece of equipment is used for hand, foot, elbow and knee combinations for power and thrust. It's great for developing shin kicking. It helps not only to condition your shins, but to take impact as well.

The Thai Pads can be stuffed with either foam or rags. Rags will form pockets from continual contact. Foam will not. They are both good. It all depends upon your preference.

These are similar to the Focus Gloves because the trainer has one for each forearm and he can maneuver them like the Focus Gloves. However, unlike Focus Gloves you can do both hand and foot combinations.

The training time is three rounds amateur and four to five rounds for the pro.

Skip ball kick-right cross-thigh kick

2

4

Right cross-left hook-thigh kick

2

4

Jab-right cross-drag up-power round kick

Right cross-left hook-power round kick

2

4

Ball kick-round kick-plant back-power round kick, using the same leg twice

Ball kick-snap back-power round kick, all done with the same leg

2

4

Skip ball
kick-round
kick-switch
power round
kick to the head

Ball kick with the back leg-step forward-power round leg

2

4

Jab-switch axe kick

Right cross-switch knee

2

Right cross-skip up knee

2

Jab-cross rear side kick-spinning back kick

Switch jab-ball kick-right cross-left hook

Jab-skip ball kick-thigh kick

2

4

Right cross-back knee-switch knee

Jab-right cross-back knee-switch-power round kick

Jab-drag side kick-spinning back kick

2

4

Switch jab-knee-back elbow

2

4

Outside thigh kick-switch-power round kick to the head

Switch jab-round kick to the head-round kick to the body

CHAPTER SIX

The Timing Ball

This piece of equipment develops your eye-hand coordination. You will improve your skills in hitting by timing your hands to the target. Use a slapping impact. Since the target is actually coming back at you it develops your blocking and bobbing as well as your timing.

Because of its fast reaction you have to work on your timing to not only move out of the way, but also meeting the target with your hands, ie. timing of the strike. Your objective is to be able to hit the Timing Ball at will. For a back and fourth reaction use the jab-right cross. For an up and down reaction practice the upper-cut. And for a side-to-side motion you will get that when you throw a left hook.

When practicing your moves, start off with one move at a time and then go into building your combinations. Remember, the harder you hit the target the quicker it reacts.

Amateurs go for three rounds and the pros four to five rounds.

Single jab

Double jab

2

Jab-left hook

2

Jab-right upper-cut-left upper cut

2

Building on your combinations.

Jab-left upper-cut- left hook

Jab-right cross-jab

2

Jab-right cross-left elbow-right elbow

Double jab-right elbow-left upper-cut-right upper-cut

Jab-bob right-come back-bob left

2

4

Jab-right cross-spinning back fist

CHAPTER SEVEN

The Jab Bag

Your first line of defense and offense is the jab. It can keep your opponent at a safe distance, at least an arms length away, and it can also be used to annoy, distract, blind (keep your glove in front of his eyes) and in some instances, do damage. Depending upon your objective at the time, it can be used to maneuver your opponent and to make him commit. In addition, if there is the slightest opening the jab can get through an opponent's defenses.

I think of it as using an artists paint brush. You can add color and style to your bout all the while you change target positions at will from the head to the body without telegraphing your intent. It is not a committed punch, so you don't leave yourself open to any offensive technique. The jab is also used to set up another punch (or kick) or a combination. With enough jabs you can wear down an opponent and after enough of them can cause damage. It's like the ancient Chinese water torture, one drop at a time in the same spot can eventually translate into those drops feeling like a sledgehammer. The same holds true to a constant jab, only magnified.

The Jab Bag is light at only 75 pounds and as such it is meant to protect your hands while you train. The jab is meant to be a snapping impact. A lighter bag teaches you how to move with it. You never start the bag in motion,

or stop it from motion by using your hands. You always use your forearms. This applies to any bag that you want to start or stop from swinging. The reason for this is you want to train yourself to treat this bag, and all bags, as if it were your opponent. If your opponent is too close for you to get off a punch, you push him out of the way by using your forearms. You wouldn't grab him by the shoulders and push him away. You wouldn't push him using your gloves because your defenses would be down. By using your forearms your defenses are always in place. The way you train is the way you react. This is true throughout your workout.

The routine for the Jab Bag is the following. Face the bag at twelve o'clock. If you go to the left you step with the left and drag with your right. Five count to the left-five count to the right-four times to the left-four times to the right-3-3,2-2 and one.

Then repeat its this time left-right-plant and jab. Now add rhythm on a five count. To the left, 1-2-3-4-5-plant-jab. Now to the right. 1-2-3-4-5- plant-jab. Four count and jab-three count and jab- two count and jab-and one.

Both amateurs and pros should do this for three rounds.

Working the jab ①

Using the Jab Bag

CHAPTER EIGHT

The Body Bag

The Body Bag is used to develop power. It weighs between 200 and 300 pounds. As you can tell it is a very heavy bag and as such it doesn't move too much. When you hit a Body Bag with a left hook, your knuckles are facing down, digging into the body. With a right cross your knuckles face up, but your motion is going down into the ribs. You don't pepper it with hits, but when you hit you give it all you've got. Each hit is a power house.

Muscles have a memory. When you go for the body it will know to give it all you've got, because that is the way you will practice. You have to expect to give more energy to a Body Bag because of its weight. That is what develops your power. As with all bags, you begin its motion and stop its motion with your forearms. Always practice as if you are really in a bout. The way you train its the way you react. Go for three rounds amateurs and pros.

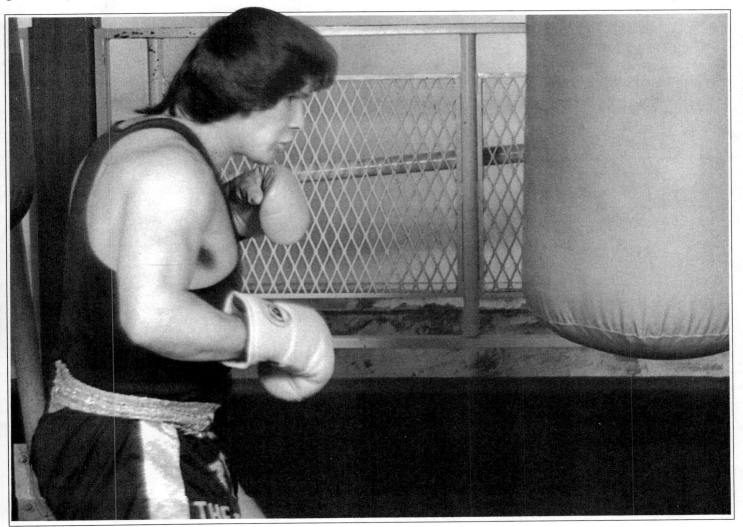

Left hook to the body - knuckles down

Right cross to the body - knuckles up

2

3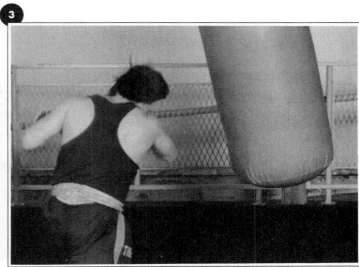

5

CHAPTER NINE

The Dancing Bag

The Dancing Bag is a 100 pound bag. It is used to find your rhythm and for giving you endurance. You use a slapping and shattering impact. It is not for a breaking impact as you would use on the Body Bag.

The routine is non-stop punching for one round, then non stop kicking for the second round if you are a kickboxer. In the third round you do a combination of both. Since it is an endurance bag you do a barrage of hitting and kicking up to the bell.

In addition you dance with it. It works this way. If the bag swings away from you, follow it without running into it, all the while you are dancing and jabbing. As it swings toward you, move back, but not out of reach for your hands and feet.

You see. what you are doing is actually dancing with the bag. When you dance with a partner the two of your can move all around the floor, gliding forward, backward, to the side, all the time maintaining the same distance from each other. The bag is your dancing partner.

As with all bags, you start and stop the action by using your forearms only. You never want to grab the bag, just as you would never grab your opponent.

This is a cardiovascular run. You are not throwing hard but you are throwing constant. Amateurs go for three rounds and pros four to five.

Push the bag with your forearm

Stopping the bag with your forearm only, always protecting your arms and shoulders. Remember to keep your opposite hand up in a defensive position.

Dancing with the bag, moving side-to-side and even putting my head on the bag as it swings, not interfering with the movement, but swaying with it as if you were dancing.

Pivot

Step-Out

Hand Technique Only

Hand and Foot Combination

Hand-Foot and Knee Combination

CHAPTER TEN

The Upper-Cut Bag

The Upper-Cut Bag is designed to develop your power, all the while it helps build your shoulders, back, wings, lower back and thighs. Your impact is an upward motion. It is usually not for the knock-out punch, but to set your opponent up for that finishing move.

You can use combinations with the Upper-Cut bag by including elbows, knees and the defensive move of weaving. Amateurs and pros both train for three rounds.

The Upper-Cut

For Knees

2

For Weaving - The bag can be stationary or it can be in motion.

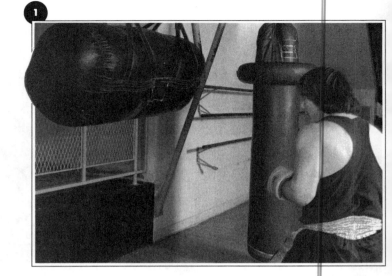

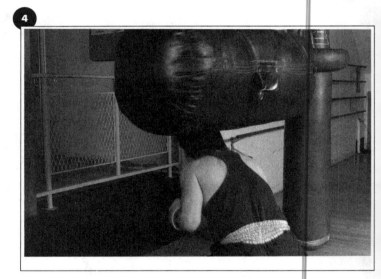

CHAPTER ELEVEN

The Banana Bag

The Banana Bag is a 300 pound bag used for target shooting. Your targets are the calf, thigh, body, chest and jaw. It develops your shin kicking. The donut around the top is used for the elbow, upper-cut, axe kick and other target areas. At 6'6" it is the tallest of all of the bags.

Hit it with a shattering impact above the waist. Below the waist use a braking impact.

Ball kick to the jaw-switch-round kick to the head

2

Ball kick-spinning back kick

2

Jab-sweep

2

Right cross-inside sweep

2

Right cross-left hook-round kick

Right cross-left hook-round kick

Jab-right cross-inside round kick

Right cross-left hook-back elbow

Jab-outside sweep-inside sweep

Jab-right upper cut-switch-round kick

3

4

CHAPTER TWELVE

The Speed Bag

The Speed Bag develops your shoulder, eye-hand coordination, hearing, rhythm and keeping your hands up even when you are tired. That is the reason for this exercise being scheduled toward the end of your work-out. You cannot hit the bag unless you keep your hands up and when a fighter is tired he tends to drop them. This exercise forces him to keep his hands raised.

Do a four count with your left, four count to your right. Then do four singles trading hands. Hear the timing of your rhythm. Every third count, hit a single slam.

With a single slam you hit the bag up against the rim. Hit with the front of your fist or the palm. Amateurs like the front of the fist because they have better control. Pros like the bottom of the fist because they can make the bag go at an angle. They do a double hit with each hand, knuckle palm-knuckle palm.

The Speed Bag comes in three sizes. The large size is a slower bag and is for beginners. The medium bag is for most of the pros and top amateurs. The peanut bag is strictly for the pro. It is the fastest of all three. Amateurs go three rounds, pros four to five.

Line the ball where the bottom of the ball is even with the tip of the nose

Straight on knuckle-palm/ straight on knuckle-palm

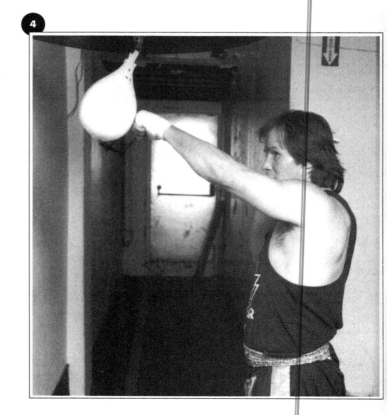

THE SLAM WEAVE

Go under the bag and slam it up against the rim

CHAPTER THIRTEEN

The Medicine Ball

he Medicine Ball ranges from five pounds to 100 pounds. It works the shoulders, legs, stomach and back for strength and endurance. It also trains the body to accept impact. It is a great all around work out. When the ball is from five to ten pounds you use one for each hand, throwing them to your partner. The ball you see in this photo session is thirty pounds.

You don't time this training by rounds, you use reps and sets. Always start moderately and build slowly.

Tightening up the muscles in your mid-section, left to right / forward and back.

Developing the stomach to take impact to the body.

Developing the sides for impact.

Developing the shoulders and back.

Developing the stomach, shoulders and back.

Developing shoulders arms, back as well as conditioning for impact.

CHAPTER FOURTEEN

The Jump Rope

This is the final exercise in the routine. It is meant for coordinating your hands and feet with rhythm, timing and developing your cardiovascular stamina. In addition, it develops the calves, thighs, stomach, shoulders, and depending upon the rope you use, the forearms.

There are strength ropes which are thick and heavy. They develop the forearms for bulk and power and weigh between one to ten pounds. There are speed ropes for a cardiovascular workout.

Your timing is different for both types of ropes. The heavier rope you time yourself by rounds. Amateurs 3 rounds, pros 6-7 rounds. The lighter rope your time is by minutes, generally 15-20 minutes.

Ropes also come in different lengths. To find your proper size you holds the handles next to both sides of your hips. The rope should just touch the floor.

The patterns are varied when you skip rope. Start your training with matador- matador-open-jump. First it's one skip at a time. Then its feet together left leg-feet together right leg. Then feet together-kick.

You develop your own patterns, always breathing through your nose. Take double short breaths in through your nose. One exhale through your mouth. If you breathe in through your mouth you'll take in too much oxygen and tire yourself. Your heart will race. You'll also dry out your mouth and get thirsty. Inhale through your nose to control your heart beat.

MATADOR

This is the same body rhythm for a right cross-left hook.
Once you've started with your Matador, then you open and begin your jump.

Feet together left leg-feet together right leg. Basic pattern.

Feet together left knee up-feet together right knee up. Same rhythm- same pattern.

CHAPTER FIFTEEN

Caring For Yourself and The Care Of Your Equipment

The Hand-Wrap

Always wrap your hands every time you train. You must protect your hands and wrists at all costs. The bones and joints are very delicate and susceptible to injury if you don't protect them.

If you start your career with that thought in mind, you will not only protect them but be protective of them as well.

There are several ways that you wrap. This is one way.

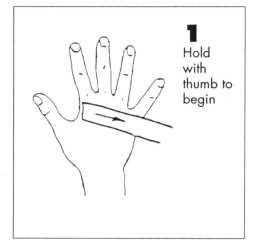

1
Hold with thumb to begin

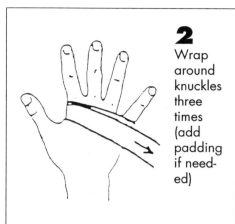

2
Wrap around knuckles three times (add padding if needed)

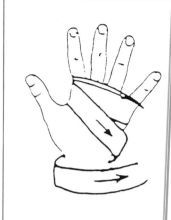

3
Across the back

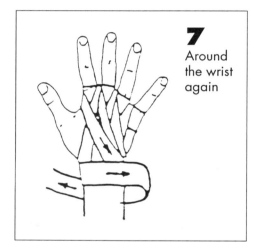

7
Around the wrist again

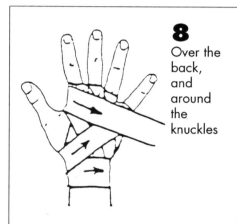

8
Over the back, and around the knuckles

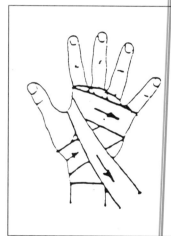

9
Around and down firmly for support

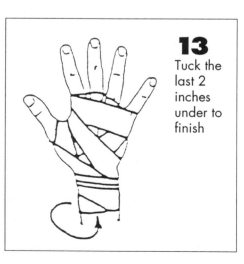

13
Tuck the last 2 inches under to finish

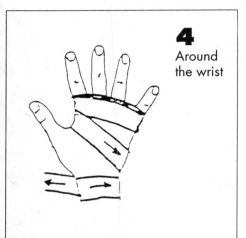

4 Around the wrist

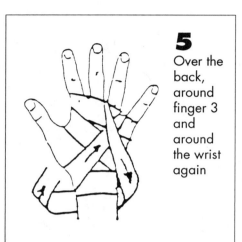

5 Over the back, around finger 3 and around the wrist again

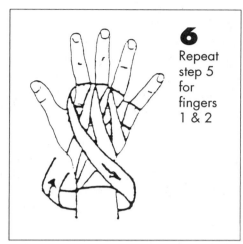

6 Repeat step 5 for fingers 1 & 2

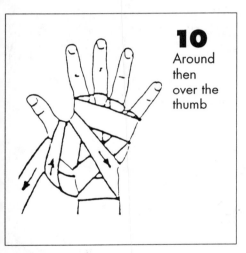

10 Around then over the thumb

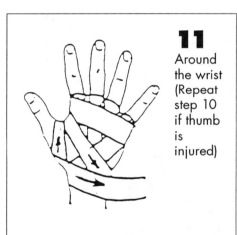

11 Around the wrist (Repeat step 10 if thumb is injured)

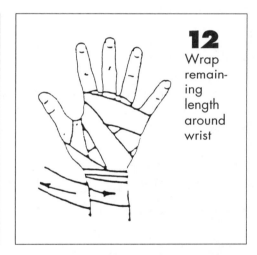

12 Wrap remaining length around wrist

If you want some extra protection, you can tape over your wraps with some boxing tape like this . . .

Start at the wrist, and go around twice, then up across the back of the hand and around the knuckles twice, then down across the back, around the wrist.

Up around the thumb

Finish at the back

If you need extra support

A fighter's hands, especially if he is good, are his weakest points. You can't build up muscle to protect these small and fragile bones. You can only care for them by wrapping them securely. You are actually bracing the wrists so they won't snap under the impact of a hit. A tremendous amount of force and pressure are concentrated into a small, relative weak area. The only way I can analogize a fighters hands is that they are like a race horses legs. They weren't designed to do what they do, so you have to compensate.

In addition, I am not only talking to the kick-boxer and boxer I am talking to my traditional martial arts friends too. When you kumite (point fight) you really should wrap your hands before you put on your free sparring gloves. I always wrapped my hands when I was doing point competition. In those days, however, we wore no gloves. So my recommendation to you is whether you wear gloves or not your best protection is the wrap.

I have had both of my hands broken several times each. Actually, I've gone into bouts with a fractured hand more than once. It was generally because of improper wrapping. I wouldn't recommend it to anyone, however I was not going to back out because of it. Being a headliner is a responsibility. Besides, I've never heard of any fighter

Shinobu Onuki Tokyo, Japan April 1978

Feint Jab. **Shinobu Onuki rematch Las Vegas, NV** January 1980

Tom Laroche Los Angeles, CA November 1985   *Photo by George Waite*

going into a competition without some aches and pains. They never go into the ring one hundred percent pain free. They just look beyond it. This is part of the passion for the ring I was talking about.

Also another word of advise to all of you martial arts practitioners. Do not train on makiwara (straw padded striking post) or practice breaking boards or bricks. This is actually supposed to demonstrate the power of the mind. This practice will damage your hands. Perhaps you won't feel it now, but later on you will. Learn to fight properly and you won't have to walk around with hands that are that toughened.

The Headgear

There is only one reason for headgear and that is to save your face from cuts and bruises. You are still going to feel the impact. You are still prone to whiplash if your neck isn't strong enough to take the impact. Having said

this I'll tell you what to look for in headgear.

For beginners and amateurs you should choose the headgear that protects the jaw (the padding and strap helps train you to keep your mouth closed), ears, cheekbones and forehead. It also has padding for the back of the head. It's not too thick, probably less than one inch. The reason you don't need a thicker one at this stage is because as a beginner or as an amateur you haven't had enough experience to hit that hard and without the experience your aim won't be that accurate.

In addition, as a beginner or amateur you only go three rounds. Once you've had the experience and you look back at new fighters you'll see how far you've come. You'll realize that at the beginning stage you really throw a lot of nothing. However, don't be discouraged, there is not a single fighter that didn't pass through this growth stage.

Top amateurs and beginning pros need a thicker headgear, probably a little over an inch thick. This will

Shinobu Onuki Tokyo, Japan April 1978

cover the cheekbones, ears and forehead. Your aim is getting more accurate so the extra padding is now needed.

With a top pro, the headgear now becomes very light. It covers a little of the cheekbones and the forehead and part of the ears. It's thick, but light. It is protecting the fighter from being cut by the jab. The jab sets the fighter up for a right cross or a left hook. This thicker headgear will absorb some of the impact from these two techniques that are now thrown with a pros authority. The pro doesn't necessarily throw harder with muscle power, but he does throw a punch more correctly, which equates to harder pound pressure. It's like driving a golf ball. Muscle power doesn't equate to distance driven. It's the authority behind the swing that counts.

In addition, a pro knows how to bob and weave so they shouldn't be getting hit as often. Pros also don't throw at random. They pick their shots.

Now there is one last type of headgear that I do not recommend, but I'm going to tell you about it anyway because you should know.

This headgear has a roll bar across the face. It's used by actors, actresses and models so their face won't be touched. They are just using it to train for a film or a photo shoot or for a little workout. On the surface this sounds like a great idea for the serious practitioner, but once I've explained it to you I think you'll agree that it's not.

You see, with that much protection the student will not have a tendency to bob and weave as much because there is not that fear of being hit in the face. However, that will not stop the neck from being snapped back or to the side after receiving the impact of a blow. All it means is that your face won't be marked and your nose won't be hit. If you don't move by using evasive techniques your neck will still take the punishment.

The way you train is the way you react. I believe you have to be on edge a little, not to the point of sheer terror mind you, but like a mild stage fright in order to make you actively involved. It is the only way you can ever hope to progress.

The Hand Wraps Material

It is just as impotant to buy the proper wraps as it is to wrap your hands correctly. It must be made of a flexible gauze-like material. A material that has some give to it. My preference are wraps that are 2 inches in width

Katsuyuki Suzuki   Tokyo, Japan August 1977

and 180 inches in length. When you wrap your hands the fingers are open. It has to be a snug secure fit. It is supposed to secure all of the joints in your hand to brace them for impact. So when you close your fingers into a fist your circulation won't be cut off. That is why you will want the wraps to have some give.

The tape that you use to secure your wraps should be cloth. You go twice around the knuckles away from the thumb. Then cross from your index finger toward your wrist. Bring around the wrist back to your pinky knuckle and then cover the knuckles for the last time. As it gets wet from sweat it will mold to your hand and form a cast to retain the shape of your fist. You will even be able to take your gloves off after your workout and keep your wraps on to continue your training. You can hit the speed bag, the timing ball, jump rope, shadow box, work on your kicks, etc. and your wraps will stay in place. You

don't want to hit a heavy bag because it will tear the skin off of your knuckles.

The Mouthpiece

The most important feature to look for in a mouthpiece is the proper fit. You want to be able to have a natural bite. If it is too big your jaw will tire and you will waste energy trying to hold on to it as well as trying to breath. If it is too small you will also waste energy trying to keep it in place. In both instances it will be dangerous to your jaw and teeth if it doesn't fit properly.

There is the double mouthpiece for the upper and lower jaws. This is good to help you control your breathing patterns. It will prevent you from breathing through your mouth, which is good. In all your training you should only breath through your nose and exhale through your mouth. There is the single for the upper jaw only. They are both good. A pro will go to the dentist and have a mouthpiece custom made.

The Boxing Shoes

The kick-boxer doesn't have to be concerned about shoes because he doesn't wear them. With the boxer the shoes have to fit properly as soon as he puts them on. He shoudn't have to break them in. There should be enough room for his feet to get wide. Like tennis shoes or track shoes there is room for expansion, the boxer needs to have that room as well. With all of that moving around his feet might tend to swell. There should be enough room so his toes don't get pinched.

The Mouthpiece and The Cup

Wrapping your hands, wearing a mouthpiece and a cup should always be worn during your workout. Why? Because the wraps lock the joints in your hands and keep them tight. This avoids damage. Secondly, it will protect your knuckles from the skin tearing off. The knuckles take a long time to heal when they are skinned and bruised because of the continual pounding they have to take during your work-out.

You should always wear a mouthpiece when you

The Weave. Howard Jackson Las Vegas, NV April 1977

Photo by Stuart Sobel

The best place to have your opponent is in the corner.
Yoshimitsu Tamashiro Tokyo, Japan October 1979

train as well as spar. Why? Because it will force you to keep your jaw closed to prevent injury. In addition it will teach you to breathe through your nose and develop breathing patterns. You'll be wearing it when you compete for real and when you spar in the gym so the more often you workout while wearing it the quicker you'll get use to it.

You should always wear a cup when you train and spar. Why? Security! It is mental and physical security. It also gets you use to wearing it and you can learn in the "tranquility" of your gym how to kick without getting bound up. You do have to make certain adjustments in your techniques and it's better to get use to these adjustment without the pressure of actual competition to contend with too. The best cup is the one that not only protects the groin, but also the bladder, liver and kidneys.

Protective Grease

Before you spar in the gym or compete in the ring your trainer will put a thin layer of Vaseline on your forehead, just above the eyebrows also on your cheeks, chin, shoulders, chest and biceps. These are all of the target areas that your opponent will be aiming for.

Shinobu Onuki   Tokyo, Japan April 1978

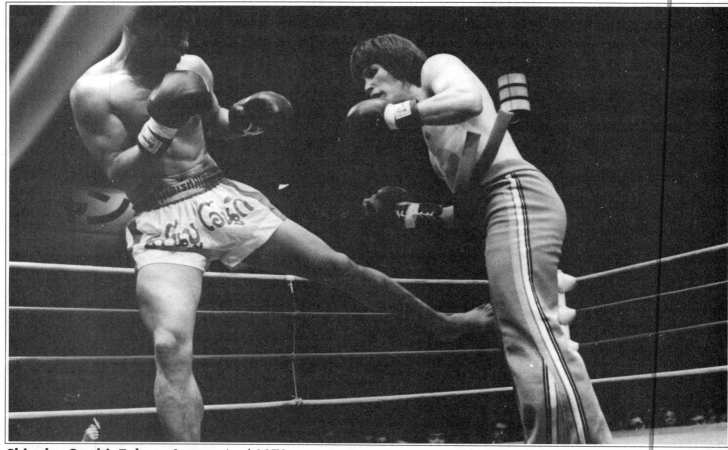

Shinobu Onuki Tokyo, Japan April 1978

The reason for Vaseline is if the skin is left dry, or with just sweat, you will be left with welts and tears wherever the body is hit. You see, when a punch is thrown the hand torques upon impact. So the body not only has to accept the hit, but also the last moment turning force. The light grease prevents this last second turn of the glove from tearing or causing unnecessary damage to the skin. Also a light film or Vaseline along the eyebrows will help to keep the sweat from running into your eyes.

The Gloves

Training gloves, also known as bag gloves are used when you do your bag work. You never want to hit the bag with gloves that you spar with. Why? Because you'll wear them out too fast and they are expensive. Bag gloves are not as expensive as sparring gloves to replace. They come in 4 oz. and 8 oz weights.

Sparring gloves come in different weights. The correct weight for you depends upon your physical weight.

The second best place to have your opponent is against the ropes. Howard Jackson Las Vegas, NV April 1977

Photo by Stuart Sobel

The following is the chart:

Up to 134 lbs. -	12 oz. gloves
135-180 lbs. -	14 oz. gloves
Over 180 lbs. -	16 oz. gloves
Super Heavy weights -	18 oz. gloves

Knock-Out Gloves. What makes one pair of 14 oz. gloves regular sparring gloves and another pair or 14 oz. gloves knock-out gloves. It is all in weight distribution and design. This is how you tell the difference. If most of the weight or padding is from the wrist to the fist they are regular gloves. However if the weight is evenly distributed from the finger tips to the forearm, it's K.O. time.

Look at the glove design. If it is well balanced it is the knock-out glove. With the knock-out gloves you have to support your hands with two inch tape criss-cross over the top of your hands and over the wraps. This better supports your wrists. You see, a knock-out glove will cause more impact to your hands and wrists as well as the increased impact to your opponent.

For regular sparring, new fighters and amateurs use safety gloves.

If you are training by yourself, look for gloves that you don't have to lace. It is generally made with velcro or elastic.

Other Things To Look For In Gloves

Your less expense gloves will generally have a seam across the striking surface. If there is any seam at all make sure it is inverted. You also want to make certain the stuffing is distributed evenly. That there are no lumps. The best gloves are made out of leather. Otherwise you will find different grades of vinyl.

Caring For Your Gloves

Make certain that you air out your gloves after your workout. The concept is the same as airing out your gym shoes. In addition, apply a light coat of Vaseline on them every other sparring session to keep them from cracking. The salt and moisture from sweat on leather or vinyl can wear and dry out your gloves.

You should not let anyone else use your sparring gloves. You want the glove to mold to your hand. If someone else uses them it will shift the padding and will become loose.

If you are the main event on a big show the promoter will sometime give each fighter a brand new pair of

identical gloves after you step into the ring. You won't have a chance to break it in so how do you quickly accomplish the break in period. What do you do? A little secret is that your corner man can take the strings after they have been half way laced on the bottom of the glove and cross them on top of the glove over the front of the knuckle and pull the leather toward the wrist. This will tighten the leather. It will become tighter than usual and will result in a more solid impact. It will mold to your fist from the sweat of your hand.

Always take care of your equipment and inspite of the hard use you'll give it they should last for a long time and give you excellent service.

Photo by Stuart Sobel

CHAPTER SIXTEEN

Benny "The Jet" Urquidez Ring Record

Compiled by Paul Maslak, Chief Administrator for the Star System

In the early days of kick-boxing in the United States, then known as *full-contact karate*, records were not kept like they are today. One of the early sanctioning bodies, the NKL (National Karate League), were city teams that traveled throughout the United States fighting other city teams. Sometimes a fighter could fight two to three times in one month. There were no Athletic Commissions to oversee what was going on. The Athletic Commissions had no idea that this was knock-out karate and not the point style tournaments that did not come under their jurisdiction. They did find out. In fact the whole country found out at the same time, as you will see later.

There was a carry-over from the point champion record keeping syndrome by fighters and promoters alike. Namely, you score the winning tournament rather than the people a competitor had to go through in order to win the title. In some of the early competition it was a point tournament structure with full-contact rules i.e., martial arts tough man contests. Official record keeping was sporadic, but Mr. Maslak, through diligent effort was able to amass as thorough a record from Benny Urquidez's career as anyone has ever been able to. While having a career as diverse as The Jet's there is bound to be controversy. You will see them duly noted below.

Benny Urquidez is the most versatile, most well traveled kickboxer in the history of the sport. He has actively gone out of his way to take on both champions and contenders alike. Going by the rules of the host country he has planted the American flag for American kick-boxers and has therefore established American fighters as some of the most innovative and talented in the world. During his twnty years of activity in the ring Urquidez has always dominated his weight division and became the World Champion of every sanctioning body he has ever fought under. The following are dates, opponents and outcomes of his bouts.

His official ring record is 58-0 with 49 KOs. The fights listed do not add up with his ring record because there were bouts that were never recorded. Karate magazines did not print every kick-boxing bout, even the major ones, therefore it was difficult then to keep as accurate record. The only thing for sure is that he has had many more fights than this record indicates. This is however, the most complete list that has ever been presented. You will now be able to follow "The Jet's" career through his three weight divisions. Note that in the early days in the Lightweight division weight was not a factor in matching opponents. For example, both Futi Semanu and Dana Goodson were 225 pounds. This was during a martial arts tough-man contest where the last man left standing wins. Until the Athletic Commission came to control the sport, over a year later, the weigh-in was anything the promoters wanted it to be. Urquidez however, was only 130 pounds when he first began to fight professionally.

The following are the outcome designations: KO - Knock-out; TKO - Technical Knock-out; KKO - Kick Knock-out; TKKO - Technical Kick Knock-out; DEC - Decision; DRW - Draw; TDRW - Technical Draw; NC - No Contest. The number after the outcome is the round number that the fight ended.

The Sanctioning Bodies: NKL - National Karate League; WPKO - World Professional Karate Organization; WSMAC - World Series of Martial Arts Championships; PKA - Professional Karate Association; WKA - World Karate Association; AJKBA - Japanese sanctioning body; KATOGI - Japanese sanctioning body; NJPW - New Japan Pro-Wrestling; MTN - Muay Thai Netherlands.

LIGHTWEIGHT DIVISION

DATE	OPPONENT	SITE	OUTCOME	SANCTION
September '74	Bill Rosehill	Honolulu, Hawaii	Win-KKO-3	WSMAC
September '74	Futi Semanu	Honolulu, Hawaii	Win-KKO-2	WSMAC
September '74	Tom Mossman	Honolulu, Hawaii	Win-THO-2	WSMAC
September '74	Burnis White	Honolulu, Hawaii	Win-KO-2	WSMAC
September '74	Dana Goodson	Honolulu, Hawaii	WIN-DEC-3	WSMAC
December '74	Burnis White	Honolulu, Hawaii	Win-KKO-4	WSMAC
February '75	Butch Bell	Atlanta, Georgia	Win-TKO-2	NKL
March '75	Ken Kolodziej	Milwaukee, Wisconsin	Win-KKO-4	NONE
March '75	Unreported	Atlanta, Georgia	Win-KKO-2	NKL
April '75	Demetrius Havanas	Dallas, Texas	Win-DEC-3	NKL
May '75	Tayari Casel	New York, New York	Win-DEC-3	WPKO
May '75	Ronald Talton	Los Angeles, California	Win-KKO-2	WSMAC
May '75	Sanun Plypoolsup	Honolulu, Hawaii	Win-TKO-2	WSMAC
June '75	Ken Riley	Honolulu, Hawaii	Win-KO-2	WSMAC
June '75	Eddie Andujar	Los Angeles, California	Win-DEC-3	NKL
July '75	Sammy Pace	Los Angeles, California	Win-KO-1	NKL
August '75	Marcelino Torres	San Juan, Puerto Rico	Win-KO-1	NKL
October '75	Bill Henderson	Los Angeles, California	Win-KO-2	WSMAC
December '75	Unreported	Detroit, Michigan	*Win-KO-2	NKL

Note:*Rules at the time required one kick for every three punches. Urquidez was disqualified for knocking his opponent out with a fourth punch. This show was aired coast to coast over network television on *ABC Sports Report*. It was a direct result of this fight that the California State Athletic Commission brought full-contact under it's protective wing. One of the problems was that any sport that can declare the person knocked-out as the winner needed looking after. Other states quickly followed suit. The NKL reinstated Urquidez's title.

early '76	Unreported	Detroit, Michigan	Win-KO-1	NKL
early '76	Ernest Hart, Jr.	Los Angeles, California	TDRW-1	NKL
June '76	Sanun Plypollsup	Dallas, Texas	Win-DEC-8	WSMAC
Late - '76	Unreported Thai	Tijuana, Mexico	Win-KKO-3	NKL
August '76	Ernest Hart, Jr.	Honolulu, Hawaii	Win-DEC-9	NKL
October '76	Eddie Andujar	Los Angeles, California	Win-TKO-8	PKA
March '77	Narong Noi	Los Angeles, California	*NC-9	WKA

Note: *In fear of a potential riot between the Thais against everyone else in the arena, the State Athletic Commission declared the fight a no-contest, in spite of Urquidez being ahead in points. A 6,000 person riot broke out anyway. This was the "cowboy era" of full-contact karate in America.

April '77	Howard Jackson	Las Vegas, Nevada	Win-TKO-4	PKA
July '77	Unreported	Mexican Tijuana, Mexico	Win-KKO-1	WKA

SUPER LIGHTWEIGHT DIVISION

August '77	Katsuyuki Suzuki	Tokyo, Japan	Win-KO-6	WKA/AJKBA
November '77	Kunimatsu Okao	Tokyo, Japan	Win-KKO-4	WKA/AJKBA
April '78	Dave Paul	Vancouver, Canada	Win-TKO-4	WKA
April '78	Takeshi Naito	Osaka, Japan	Win-KKO-1	KATOGI
May '78	Shinobu Onuki	Tokyo, Japan	Win-TKO-2	WKA/AJKBA
August '78	Unreported Thai	Tokyo, Japan	*NC-6	KATOGI

Note: *Urquidez had agreed to make a publicity appearance at this event. However, when one of the semi-main events fell through, he agreed to perform a *no-decision* exhibition under kick-boxing rules (with elbows). At the end of the bout a decision was given to Urquidez's opponent in an effort to embarrass KATOGI's rival AKJKBA organization in spite of the agreement being a No Contest. The judges decision was overruled.

May '79	Rick Simmerly	Lake Tahoe, Nevada	Win-KO-6	WKA
September '79	Frank Holloway	Ensenada, Mexico	Win-DEC-9	WKA
October '79	Yoshimitsu Tamashiro	Tokyo, Japan	Win-DEC-9	WKA
January '80	Shinobu Onuki	Las Vegas, Nevada	Win-KO-7	WKA
April '80	Frank Holloway	Vancouver, Canada	Win-DEC-9	WKA
August '80	Billye Jackson	Palm Beach, Florida	*NC-7	WKA

Note: *Jackson, a last minute replacement for what was supposed to be non-title bout, told the promoter in the dressing room just prior to his bout that he would not fight if Urquidez was allowed to use leg kicks. Leg kicks is a rule which the WKA made mandatory in order for it's bouts to be sanctioned with International Rules. To please the crowd that had come to see Urquidez fight, his first time in Florida, he agreed not to kick to Jackson's legs, in spite of having trained for leg kicks.

Unintentionally, Urquidez did use leg kicks several time. "The way you train is the way you react". The center referee deducted points without giving any warning and threatened Urquidez with disqualification. The judges added the score at the end of the bout and said Jackson won. The judges score cards "mysteriously" disappeared as did the video when a protest was lodged by the Urquidez camp. Because of so many irregularities that surrounded this bout, the board of directors of the WKA declared the fight a No Contest (NC). Jackson was given the opportunity to fight Urquidez again, this time for his title, but neither Jackson nor his camp would ever agree.

April '81	Kong Fu Tak	Hong Kong, China	Win-TKKO-4	WKA
June '82	Yutaka Koshikawa	Vancouver, Canada	Win-TKKO-6	WKA
January '83	Kunimasa Nagae	Tokyo, Japan	Win-KO-4	WKA
September '83	Iron Fujimoto	Tokyo, Japan	Win-KO-6	WKA

WELTERWEIGHT DIVISION

January '84	Iwan Sprang	Amsterdam, Holland	Win-TKO-6	MTN
November '85	Tom Laroche	Los Angeles, California	Win-DEC-12	WKA
April '89	Nobuya Azuka	Tokyo, Japan	Win-DEC-5	AJPW

RETIREMENT BOUT

December '93	Yoshihisa Tagami	Las Vegas, Nevada	Win-SPLIT-DEC	WKA

Photo by Stuart Sobel

RETIREMENT BOUT: At the age of 41 Benny Urquidez retires after winning a very tough bout against a 25 year old Japanese champion Yoshihisa Tagami with a 22-0 record going into the fight.

The Urquidez reign spans 20 years from the very inception of kick-boxing in America, then called full-contact karate. He was stripped of his world title once by the Professional Karate Association (PKA) because of his renegade ways (he wouldn't sign an exclusive agreement with them), but he never relinquished it in the ring.

He is a true American martial arts pioneer in the sport of kick-boxing. His legacy to the sport is it's history and all of the Jet Fighters that he has spawned. His analytical approach to a very tough game gives credence to the view point that the sport truly is a science, the sweet science of fighting.

Photos by Stuart Sobel

The Okao Bout

'My toughest opponent was Kunimatsu Okao. I give him all the respect. He really put me on my game. Even though I knocked him out in four rounds, it was one heck of a four rounds. He was a fabulous chess player. See INTRODUCTION for explanation of chess player.

Some historical background.

The first time Benny Urquidez fought in Japan it was in August of 1977 against the great champion Katsuyuki Suzuki. When Suzuki was knocked out in the sixth round, with numerous standing eight counts I might add, (the referee and judges didn't want him to lose) Okao challenged him on the spot while he was still in the ring. Urquidez took that

challenge in November of the same year. You see, Okao was a champion who retired undefeated. He had groomed his top student Suzuki to take the championship title, which he did.

Urquidez then came to Tokyo with a troup of American fighters. They were all supposed to fight contenders. Urquidez was thrown a ringer by being given a champion. No one read or spoke Japanese so no one from the U.S. knew.

Not only did he win his bout with Suzuki, he was the only one on the American team to do so. It was because of this win that American fighters were asked back. For this reason Urquidez has been called "the Marco Polo of American kick-boxing". He single-handedly opened the gateway to the Orient for American fighters.

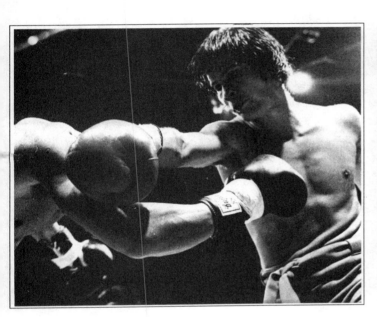

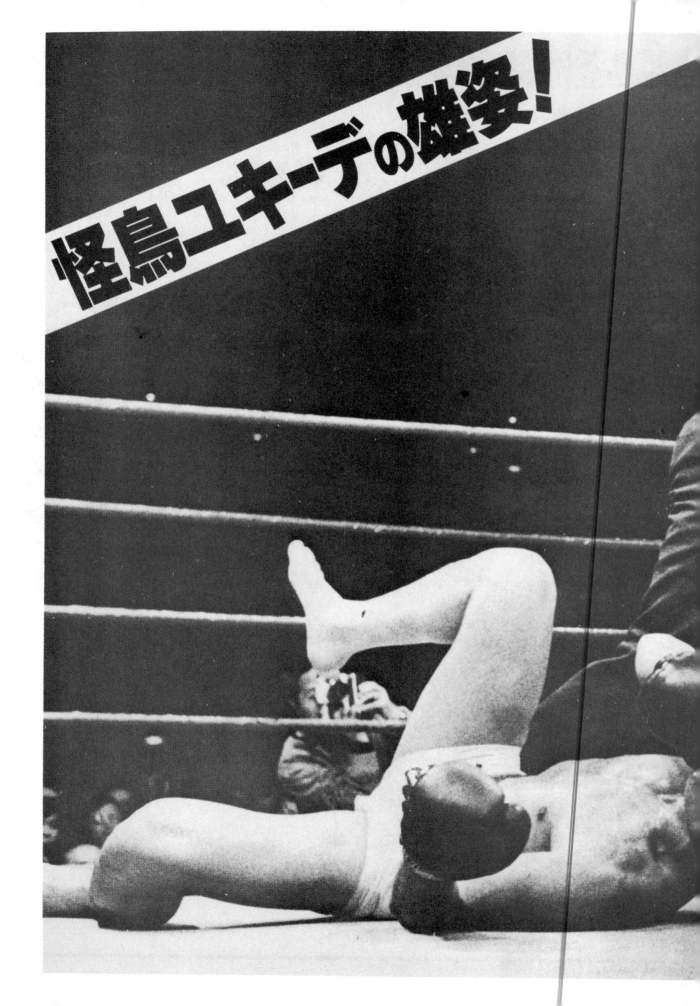

怪鳥コキーデの雄姿！

'77 11/14 対岡尾国光戦・日本武道館